Sonia Sotomayor

Sonia Sotomayor
From the Bronx
to the US Supreme Court

LIZ SONNEBORN

LERNER PUBLICATIONS ◆ MINNEAPOLIS

To Linda, mother-in-law extraordinaire

Lerner Publications Company
An imprint of Lerner Publishing Group, Inc.
241 First Avenue North
Minneapolis, MN 55401 USA

For reading levels and more information, look up this title at www.lernerbooks.com.

Main body text set in Rotis Serif Std.
Typeface provided by Adobe Systems.

Designer: Connie Kuhnz

Library of Congress Cataloging-in-Publication Data

Names: Sonneborn, Liz, author.
Title: Sonia Sotomayor : from the Bronx to the US Supreme Court / Liz Sonneborn.
Description: Minneapolis, MN : Lerner Publications Company, [2024] | Series: Gateway
  biographies | Includes bibliographical references and index. | Audience: Ages 9–14 |
  Audience: Grades 4–6 | Summary: "Sonia Sotomayor, associate justice to the US Supreme
  Court, is known for her straightforward approach and efforts toward equality. Learn about her
  road to the Supreme Court and over ten years of work"– Provided by publisher.
Identifiers: LCCN 2022051904 (print) | LCCN 2022051905 (ebook) | ISBN 9781728491769
  (library binding) | ISBN 9798765602966 (paperback) | ISBN 9781728497624 (ebook)
Subjects: LCSH: Sotomayor, Sonia, 1954–Juvenile literature. | Judges–United States–
  Biography–Juvenile literature. | United States. Supreme Court–Biography–Juvenile literature.
Classification: LCC KF8745.S67 S66 2024 (print) | LCC KF8745.S67 (ebook) | DDC 347.73/2634
  [B]–dc23/eng20230224

LC record available at https://lccn.loc.gov/2022051904
LC ebook record available at https://lccn.loc.gov/2022051905

Manufactured in the United States of America
1-53115-51125-2/23/2023

TABLE OF CONTENTS

Sotomayor promotes her book *Turning Pages: My Life Story.*

In 1990 Sonia Sotomayor walked into her office at the prestigious law firm of Pavia & Harcourt and found a surprise waiting for her. It was an application for a federal judgeship from Senator Daniel Patrick Moynihan of New York's congressional committee, which searched for and selected judicial candidates.

Sotomayor was excited but a little stunned. Since she was a girl, she had wanted to be a judge. But it always seemed like an impossible dream. She was a Latina from a working-class background. People like her rarely held judgeships.

Justice Sotomayor on the United States Supreme Court in 2009

She grabbed the application and walked down the hall to the office of her colleague Dave Botwinik to get his opinion. He urged her to fill it out. He told her the committee wanted to diversify the federal judiciary—the judges that work in the federal court system. The committee was looking for qualified Hispanic candidates.

The application was extremely long. She had to provide details about every aspect of her adult life. Sotomayor knew the committee was looking for unethical behaviors that would disqualify candidates for the job. She was confident they would not find any in her application. With the idea of becoming a judge always in the back of her mind, she had been careful to make ethical decisions throughout her life.

A couple of weeks after Sotomayor submitted the application, the committee scheduled an interview. Even though she doubted she would get the job, she threw herself into preparing for the meeting. She sought out the advice of every lawyer she knew about the judicial nomination process. She tried to guess what questions she might be asked and prepared a well-thought-out answer for each one.

On the day of the interview, Sotomayor walked into a conference room where about fifteen people, mostly male lawyers, were sitting around a table. They began bombarding her with questions, but she had quick and clear answers for all of them. Then she was asked the one question she had not anticipated: "Don't you think learning to be a judge will be hard for you?"

She had no trouble answering. After taking a short breath, she said, "I've spent my whole life learning how to do things that were hard for me. None of it has ever been easy." She explained that even though she did not come from a privileged background, she had earned college and law degrees from some of the best schools in the country. She had also had an excellent career as an assistant district attorney and a copyright lawyer. "[W]herever I've gone, I've honestly never felt fully prepared at the outset," she told the group. "Yet each time I've survived, I've learned, and I've thrived."

Soon after the interview, Senator Moynihan requested a private meeting. They chatted for over an hour before the conversation wound down. Sotomayor expected weeks of nervously waiting for word about how the meeting had gone. But on the spot, Moynihan said he was nominating her for the US District Court. Before he did, though, he wanted to know whether she was prepared to spend her professional life as a judge.

It was the easiest question of all. "Yes!" she said.

Since then, Sonia Sotomayor has devoted herself to serving as a judge in the federal court system. After years on a district court, she was promoted to the US Court of Appeals. Then in 2009 she became an associate justice of the Supreme Court, the highest court of the United States. While making rulings on the most important issues of the day, she also made history as the Supreme Court's first Hispanic and third female justice.

In the Bronx

Sonia Maria Sotomayor was born on June 25, 1954, in the Bronx, one of the five boroughs, or political divisions, of New York City. About ten years earlier, her mother, Celina, and her father, Juan, had moved to the Bronx from Puerto Rico.

Sonia's family lived in the Bronxdale Houses. This housing project made up of red-brick buildings was owned by the city. Most of the adults living in Bronxdale were working class, including Sonia's parents. Juan worked in a factory. Celina worked first as a telephone operator and later as a nurse.

Growing up, Sonia was surrounded by family. In addition to her little brother, Juan, her playmates included many cousins. She was also very close to her grandmother, who lived in her own apartment nearby.

A family photograph of Sonia (*center*) and her parents

On Saturday nights, Sonia and her relatives gathered at her grandmother's. The smell of garlic and onion filled the air as her grandmother cooked Sonia's favorite Puerto Rican dishes. Everyone feasted and played games of dominos as Sonia's step-grandfather played his güiro, a guitar-like instrument. Late into the night, they all fell silent as her grandmother recited poetry in Spanish. Although some of Sonia's relatives were fluent in English, they always spoke Spanish at home.

For these parties, Sonia dressed in her nicest clothes. But her dress always ended up wrinkled or stained. Sonia's family nicknamed her Aji, meaning hot pepper, because she could barely sit still. Her mother complained that she was always running around and never seemed to stop talking.

Sonia was eager to jump into anything and take control. That attitude helped her deal with several difficult moments during her childhood. When she was seven, she was diagnosed with diabetes, a condition that affects the amount of sugar in a

A young Sonia

person's blood. Her family was very upset, so Sonia knew her condition was serious. To stay alive and healthy, she would have to be injected every day with insulin, which helps control blood sugar. Even though she was afraid of shots, Sonia insisted on learning how to inject the insulin herself. She later said that living with diabetes taught her self-discipline early in life.

While her parents loved her very much, Sonia's home life was often hard. Her mother and father fought frequently, usually over her father's excessive drinking. Celina started working nights just so she could avoid spending time with her husband. When the tension in her household became too much, Sonia escaped to her grandmother's apartment for some peace and quiet.

When Sonia was eight, her father died suddenly. Her mother began working long hours to keep the family afloat. Left alone with her grief, Sonia turned to books for comfort. She loved reading about the Greek gods. She learned from the stories that *Sonia* was a version of the name Sophia, which meant wisdom. Sonia also enjoyed mysteries featuring the girl detective Nancy Drew.

About the same time, Sonia became a driven student. Her teacher gave out gold stars for good work. That ignited Sonia's competitive streak. She worked hard at school to get more gold stars.

Sonia's mother was pleased. She told her children they needed a good education to be successful adults. She bought her children a set of the *Encyclopedia Britannica.* The books contained general knowledge about many different topics. If people had a question about something, such as a sport or a historical event, they could find information about it there. Both Sonia and Juan pored over the books, eager to learn everything they could.

When Sonia was ten, she discovered what she wanted to do with her life. The answer did not come from a teacher or a book, but from a television show. She loved

Perry Mason ran on the television network CBS from 1957 to 1966.

watching *Perry Mason*, a drama about a heroic lawyer. Every week, he ended up in a courtroom defending someone wrongly accused of a crime.

Sonia was fascinated by the arguments the lawyers made on the show. But she was even more interested by the judges who oversaw the trials. She could see that the judge was the most important person in the courtroom. No one she knew was a lawyer, much less a judge. But, as impossible as her dream seemed, she was determined to become one.

School Days

In high school, Sonia began to plot a course toward her goal. She knew she would have to go first to college and then to law school. But before then, she had work to do.

Sonia graduates from eighth grade.

For first through eighth grade, she had gone to a private Catholic school. The nuns who taught there made the students memorize facts. To get good grades, all students had to do was repeat those facts.

To make it to law school, though, Sonia realized she needed to learn how to think through an idea and make an argument. Sonia joined her high school debate club. The club members competed with other schools. Each team tried to make the best speeches about social and political issues. Sonia became a star debater. In just a few minutes, she could craft a convincing argument in favor of or against any topic.

High school was not all work for Sonia. She had many friends, both on and off the debate team. Her family had moved to a larger apartment in the new Co-op City housing complex. Their kitchen table became a popular place for her classmates to meet after school for snacks and conversation.

During her senior year, one of Sonia's former fellow debaters encouraged her to apply to Ivy League schools. After all, she was the valedictorian—the leading student—of her class. He gave her a list of top colleges to research, including Princeton University in New Jersey. She applied to Princeton and was awarded a scholarship.

Sotomayor struggled to adjust at Princeton. The university had just started admitting women, and there were very few students of color. Some students and faculty were hostile toward Sotomayor because she was Latina. They thought only white men should be allowed to attend the school.

Sotomayor's 1976 Princeton yearbook photo

Sotomayor also struggled with her classwork. She realized that her English skills were not as polished as those of most other students because she grew up speaking a lot of Spanish. To become a better writer, she studied English grammar books on her own time. She also improved her vocabulary by learning ten new words each day.

As her confidence grew, Sotomayor joined Acción Puertorriqueña, a Puerto Rican student group. The organization wanted Princeton to hire Hispanic professors or administrators. Sotomayor helped file a formal complaint with the federal government. The university responded by hiring a Hispanic man as the assistant dean of student affairs.

Despite the challenges she faced, Sotomayor was successful at Princeton. She won the Moses Taylor Pyne Honor Prize, the university's highest award for a graduating senior. After graduating, she married Kevin Noonan, who she had been dating since high school. Sotomayor then set her sights on Yale University. Its law school was one of the best in the country.

Sotomayor did well at Yale. She was an editor of the *Yale Law Journal.* She was also the managing editor of *Yale Studies in World Public Order.* Her grades and achievements could have earned her a spot in a leading law firm with an impressive salary. But unlike many of her classmates, she wanted more than just a high-status, high-paying job.

She found what she was looking for when the District Attorney (DA) of New York County, Robert M. Morgenthau,

District Attorney Robert M. Morgenthau in a New York City courtroom

visited Yale. He was recruiting students to join his office. Few Yale students were interested because the pay was relatively low for graduates of a top law school. But Sotomayor jumped at the chance. The job would let her immediately get experience trying cases in a courtroom.

Learning the Ropes

The staff at the Manhattan District Attorney's office had a nickname for young, inexperienced lawyers like Sotomayor. They called them ducklings. Ducklings were often overwhelmed by the chaotic atmosphere. The

DA prosecuted all types of crimes—from shoplifting to murder. Because New York was experiencing a crime wave in the 1980s, the workload was crushing.

Sotomayor threw herself into being an assistant DA. In the courtroom, she made cases against criminal suspects. It was her job to convince a jury to return a guilty verdict.

Sotomayor was devastated when she lost two of her early felony cases. She went to her boss and asked what she was doing wrong. He said she had done a good job building a logical case. But she had not made an emotional connection with the jury. He explained that most people did not like sending a suspect to jail. They only found people guilty if they felt in their hearts that it was the right thing to do.

Sotomayor was relieved. Her law school years taught her how to carefully build an argument. But she was naturally good at reading people and appealing to their emotions. After her boss's lesson, she never again lost a case.

As a duckling, Sotomayor mostly prosecuted petty crimes, working as many as eighty cases at a time. But once she proved herself, she was assigned to more important criminal trials. One of the most newsworthy was the Tarzan Murderer case. Richard Maddicks was accused of using a rope to swing, like the movie character Tarzan, into top-story apartments from rooftops and other buildings. While robbing apartments, he shot anyone who interrupted him. Sotomayor helped secure a guilty verdict and a long prison sentence for Maddicks.

During her time at the DA's office, Sotomayor often worked fifteen hours a day. She had almost no time for a personal life. She barely saw her husband, who was busy earning an advanced degree at Princeton. Eventually they realized they had grown apart and decided to get a divorce in 1983.

Sotomayor's job was also taking a toll on her spirit. She had always had faith in people and looked for the best in them. But being a prosecutor trained her to see the worst in criminal suspects. She recognized that the work often made prosecutors become more negative over time. She decided to leave the DA's office when she "could see the signs that I too was hardening, and I didn't like what I saw."

Sotomayor had another reason for changing careers. She still dreamed of becoming a judge, and prosecutors were rarely nominated for judgeships. To be a judge, she also needed to know more about civil law, which deals with legal disputes between individuals or organizations.

With that goal in mind, Sotomayor joined the private law firm of Pavia & Harcourt in 1984. Its elegant New York offices were a far cry from the dank, crowded DA's office. Many of her clients made expensive handbags and watches. Sotomayor brought lawsuits against people who made cheap copies of their goods. The work paid well, and her colleagues and clients respected her. After 1988, when she was made a partner of the firm, she could have stayed in this comfortable job for the rest of her working days. But when she received an application for a federal judgeship two years later, it was an opportunity too good to pass up. Finally, it looked as though her childhood dream might come true.

Sotomayor in her office overlooking the old Federal Courthouse on Foley Square after joining the United States Court of Appeals in 1998

Holding Court

After Sotomayor was nominated to be a district court judge, she had to go before the US Senate for a confirmation hearing. The hearing was like a job interview, with members of the Senate asking probing questions about her career and qualifications. To her great relief, the hearing was a breeze. She had the support of both George H. W. Bush, the Republican president, and Daniel Patrick Moynihan, an influential Democratic senator. Senators from both political parties came together after the hearing to confirm her nomination with a unanimous vote.

In October 1992, Sotomayor joined the Southern District of New York. She was the youngest federal judge in the district. Between 1992 and 1998, she presided over about 450 trials.

In June 1997, President Bill Clinton nominated Sotomayor to the US Court of Appeals for the Second Circuit. It was a promotion to a higher court. Appeals

Sotomayor converses with her former law clerk Melissa Murray at an event in Berkeley, California, in 2017.

courts examine whether the law was applied properly in decisions made by lower courts. Instead of presiding over jury trials, she would be part of a three-judge panel that would decide each case.

Rush Limbaugh, a popular conservative radio host, opposed her nomination. He said that her elevation to the appeals court would mean that the liberal-leaning Sotomayor might soon be nominated to the Supreme Court. In response, conservative politicians slowed the nomination process. Finally in October 1998, Sotomayor got her Senate hearing. Her nomination was approved with a vote of 67–29.

Sotomayor served almost seventeen years as a district and appeals court judge. During that time, she developed a reputation for paying close attention to details. According to Adam Abensohn, who worked for her as a clerk, "She takes each case and works it to death to get the right result." She also expected lawyers to come to court well-prepared and openly criticized them when they were not.

Although Sotomayor was tough on ill-prepared lawyers, she was very popular with the clerks she hired to assist her. She often invited them to her home for parties or movie nights. She also took an interest in their careers and personal lives, treating them more like family members than employees.

Some judges insert witty remarks or showy language in their writings about a case. Sotomayor preferred a much more direct writing style. She wanted her ideas

The Savior of Baseball

When Sotomayor was a district court judge, she presided over a dispute between Major League Baseball players and team owners. Looking for a better financial deal, the players went on strike. They refused to play for 232 days, halting the 1994 season. Sotomayor sided with the players and ordered that an old contract could stay in place as the two sides worked toward a new one. The players ended their strike, and baseball fans everywhere hailed Sotomayor as the savior of baseball.

to be clear not just to lawyers and judges, but also to the public. Her former clerk Melissa Murray explained, "Her principal concern, beyond getting it right, was that opinions were explained in a way ordinary people will understand."

Sotomayor was also known for her practical approach to the law. Like any good judge, her decisions were rooted in a careful review of the law. But she rarely failed to examine the real-life consequences of her rulings. As a district and appeals court judge, Sotomayor was mindful of how the legal system could affect ordinary people for better or for worse.

The 111th Justice

On the evening of May 25, 2009, Sonia Sotomayor nervously awaited news that could change the course of her life. Shortly after 8:00 p.m., her cell phone rang. When she answered, she heard the voice of President Barack Obama. He said he was going to nominate Sotomayor to the Supreme Court of the United States. She burst into tears.

Obama's search for a new Supreme Court justice began just weeks before, when Justice David Souter announced his retirement. The president and his advisers came up with four candidates, including Sotomayor. She had ample experience for the job. She had had an excellent education and a rich and varied legal career. But to many court-watchers, she seemed like a long shot because she was the only candidate Obama had never met.

The president interviewed all four candidates. During his session with Sotomayor, she performed so well she became his favorite. Her personal story appealed to Obama. He was particularly impressed that, despite her great success, she kept close ties to the neighborhood where she grew up.

On May 26, the president formally announced Sotomayor as his nominee. He praised her intelligence and knowledge of the law. But he also hailed her evolution from being a working-class girl in a Bronx housing project to a justice on the highest court of the land. He said, "It is experience that can give a person a common touch and a sense of compassion, an understanding of how the world works and how ordinary people live."

Obama announces his nomination of Sotomayor to the US Supreme Court on May 26, 2009.

The US Senate had to vote on Sotomayor's nomination before she could join the Supreme Court. But first she had to be interviewed by senators in three days of public hearings. As a nominee of a Democratic president, she was likely to get votes from all sixty Democratic senators. Their votes were enough to ensure her confirmation. But she hoped to win over some Republican senators as well. She scheduled meetings with senators from both parties. Even though she was on crutches after breaking her ankle, she managed to meet with ninety-two out of one hundred senators.

White House staffers spent weeks grilling Sotomayor. They wanted to prepare her for questions from senators who opposed the president. Meanwhile, newspaper and magazine articles suggested what lines of attack they might use. One of the most read was called "The Case Against Sotomayor." Its author, Jeffrey Rosen, quoted an anonymous source that said Sotomayor was "not that smart and kind of a bully on the bench."

The criticism deeply hurt Sotomayor. She later said, "It was very, very painful . . . on the Supreme Court

Sonia from the Block

Some of Sonia Sotomayor's clerks jokingly call her Sonia from the Block. The nickname is a play on "Jenny from the Block," a 2002 hit song by singer and movie star Jennifer Lopez. In the lyrics, Lopez says that, for all her fame, she is still the same person she was as a young Latina growing up in the working-class Bronx. In many speeches and public appearances, Sotomayor has said the same thing about herself.

Sotomayor meets with Senator Jeff Sessions, a member of the Republican Party, on June 2, 2009, prior to her confirmation hearing.

nomination process that people kept accusing me of not being smart enough." She believed people only said that because she was Hispanic. In 2019 Rosen apologized to Sotomayor for his article.

Obama's opponents also criticized Sotomayor for a speech she often gave to groups of Hispanic lawyers and students. Her speech was meant to inspire them to have faith in themselves. In it, she said that a "wise Latina woman . . . would more often than not reach a better conclusion than a white male" who had not had her life experiences.

On July 13, 2009, the confirmation hearing began. Sotomayor answered the senators' questions carefully and calmly. Her manner challenged the idea that she was too emotional or impatient to serve on the court. She reassured her critics that she would make judicial decisions only by applying the law and that her personal views would not influence her rulings.

Sotomayor testifies before the Senate Judiciary Committee during her confirmation hearing.

On August 6, the Senate held the vote. Sixty-eight senators, including nine Republicans, voted to confirm her nomination. Two days later, Sotomayor was sworn in as the 111th justice of the US Supreme Court.

On the Bench

The Supreme Court of the United States is at the top of the federal court system. Most of its cases are appeals to overturn a ruling of a lower court. Each year, the nine justices on the court receive about seven thousand requests to reexamine a court decision. They can only take on about one hundred per term, which runs from early October to late June. The justices choose cases that will have the greatest impact on American society.

During oral arguments, lawyers make their case to the justices, who might ask questions about the lawyers' legal reasoning. The justices then privately vote on the case. Those in majority issue a written opinion to the public explaining their decision. Justices in the minority can issue a dissent to spell out why they disagree.

When justices first join the court, they usually hold back a little until they have proven themselves to their colleagues. Sotomayor, though, was an active participant in oral arguments from her first case. From day one, she signaled that she was going to be an assertive force on the court.

Sotomayor has generally been a liberal-leaning justice. Consistent with liberal views, she was in the minority of

A Colorful Justice

Sotomayor's nomination process was so tightly controlled that White House staffers advised her on how to dress. To play it safe, they picked out a beige suit for her swearing-in ceremony. It was so plain that no one could criticize it. They even told her to paint her fingernails a neutral color.

After Sotomayor was confirmed, she attended a celebration in her honor. She asked Obama if he noticed anything different about her. She then held up her hands, showing off her newly painted, bright-red fingernails.

her first important case, *Citizens United v. Federal Election Commission* (2010). The conservative majority of the court ruled that corporations could spend unlimited amounts of money on election campaigns. In another far-reaching case, *Obergefell v. Hodges* (2015), Sotomayor was in the majority. The court's decision legalized same-sex marriage in all fifty states.

Throughout her career on the Supreme Court, Sotomayor has shown a strong interest in criminal justice reform and defendants' rights. One of her most spirited dissents was in *Billy Ray Irick v. Tennessee* (2018). She objected to the execution of a prisoner by a drug that could cause extreme pain. Sotomayor wrote that if the court allowed the execution, "we have stopped being a civilized nation."

Sotomayor has also been a vigorous defender of the rights of women and of racial and ethnic groups that have faced discrimination. She is particularly a champion of affirmative action, which the court has examined in many cases. Affirmative action programs favor people from groups that historically have been discriminated against. Although Sotomayor did not know it at the time, she was admitted to Princeton in part because the university's affirmative action program was seeking more Hispanic students. She has frequently

A Controversial Case

During her time on the appeals court, Sotomayor heard more than three thousand cases. The most controversial was *Ricci v. DeStefano*. A group of mostly white firefighters sued New Haven, Connecticut. Fire department officials had thrown out test results that qualified the firefighters for promotions because Black firefighters had not done as well on the test. Sotomayor and the two other judges upheld a lower court ruling approving the city's actions. The decision was widely criticized and later overturned by the Supreme Court on June 29, 2009.

On June 26, 2015, James Obergefell (*bottom center*) gives a speech to the media after the US Supreme Court's ruling in favor of same-sex marriage.

praised affirmative action, explaining that it gave her many opportunities she otherwise would not have had.

Although Sotomayor often uses blunt language in oral arguments and in dissents, she has made friendly relationships with the other justices on the Court. She has publicly highlighted her friendship with conservative justice Clarence Thomas. In a 2022 speech, she said, "I think we share a common understanding about people and kindness towards them. That's why I can be friends with him and still continue our daily battle over our difference of opinions in cases."

Sotomayor has also worked to develop a strong connection with the public. While a Supreme Court justice, she has delivered hundreds of speeches at schools, universities, and lawyers' organizations. She often tells stories from her own life to inspire young people, particularly students of color, to pursue their goals.

Sotomayor delivers a speech to students in Denver, Colorado, in 2010.

The Judge of Sesame Street

Sotomayor's many television appearances include two visits to *Sesame Street*. In one, she resolves a dispute between Goldilocks and Baby Bear. In the other, she explains to Muppet Abby Cadabby what a career is. At first, Abby wants to be a princess, but she then decides to become a judge like her friend Sonia.

Unlike most justices, Sotomayor has been open about her personal life. In 2013 she published an intimate memoir titled *My Beloved World*, in which she discussed her insecurities. The popular book became a national bestseller. Sotomayor has also written the children's books *Turning Pages: My Life Story* in 2018, *Just Ask! Be Different, Be Brave, Be You* in 2019, and *Just Help! How to Build a Better World* in 2022.

Sotomayor has traveled the country, visiting with fans of her books at bookstore events. She also has frequently appeared on television shows, including *The Today Show* and *The View*. She even joined many celebrities on live television to oversee the dropping of the New Year's Eve ball in Times Square in 2013. Her outgoing nature and eagerness to meet with the public has earned Sotomayor the nickname the People's Justice.

Sotomayor holds her book *Just Help! How to Build a Better World* in front of the Capitol Building.

In the Minority

Serving on the Supreme Court is a lifetime appointment. Justices leave the job by choosing to retire, being removed, or dying. Because justices often serve together for decades, they work hard to get along. They observe traditions like shaking hands before hearing a case. They frequently gather for informal lunches and celebrate one another's birthdays together.

But during the presidency of Donald Trump, the relations between the justices became strained. President

Trump selected three new Supreme Court justices. Like Trump, all three held conservative views. At the end of his presidency, six of the court's justices were considered conservative. Only three, including Sotomayor, were considered liberal.

In this new court, the three-justice liberal minority has little power. The conservative justices can decide which cases the court will hear or not hear without the input of the other three justices. They may also rule in favor of decisions that favor conservative beliefs.

Official photo of the Supreme Court taken on October 7, 2022

For example, with its ruling on *Dobbs v. Jackson Women's Health Organization* in 2022, the court allowed states to ban abortion. During the oral arguments for Dobbs, Sotomayor strongly criticized the case. She pointed out that the right to an abortion, established nearly fifty years earlier by the 1973 case *Roe v. Wade*, had been upheld by fifteen Supreme Court justices from all different backgrounds. She suggested that if the conservative justices ruled in favor of Dobbs, they would be following their political beliefs instead of interpreting the law.

Sotomayor's bronze bust stands at the Bronx Terminal Market.

On June 30, 2022, Justice Stephen Breyer retired. Sotomayor then became the liberal justice who had served on the court the longest. She had a new responsibility. When the court rules with the conservative justices on one side and the liberal justices on the other, she chooses which liberal justice writes the dissent.

Sotomayor has also written dissents for cases she thinks the court should hear but that the conservative justices have rejected. These dissents do not affect the law in the present. But they may persuade a future court to take another look at these cases.

Of the three liberal justices, Sotomayor has been the most vocal critic of the court's actions and decisions since Trump's presidency. On June 16, 2022, she vented her frustration in a speech to the American Constitution Society. "There are moments where I am deeply, deeply disappointed," she said.

In the same speech, though, Sotomayor expressed her confidence in the Supreme Court as an institution. "We have to have continuing faith in the court system [and] in our system of government," she maintained. With the determination that took her from the Bronx to the Supreme Court, she also declared her commitment to the rule of law and the quest for justice. "[Y]es, there have been moments where I've stopped and said, 'Is this worth it anymore?'" Sotomayor confessed. But she added, "[E]very time I do that, I lick my wounds for a while . . . And then I say, OK—let's fight."

IMPORTANT DATES

1954   Sonia Maria Sotomayor is born.

1962   She is diagnosed with type 1 diabetes at seven years old.

1972   Sotomayor graduates first in her class from Cardinal Spellman High School.

1976   She graduates with honors from Princeton University.

She marries her longtime boyfriend, Kevin Noonan.

1979   Sotomayor earns a law degree from Yale Law School.

She joins the New York County District Attorney's office.

1983   Sotomayor and Noonan divorce.

1984   Sotomayor joins the law firm Pavia & Harcourt.

1992   She becomes a judge on the US District Court for the Southern District of New York.

1995   She "saves" baseball with a ruling that ends a Major League Baseball strike.

1998   Sotomayor becomes a judge on the US Court of Appeals for the Second Circuit.

2009   She becomes an associate justice of the Supreme Court of the United States.

2013   She publishes her memoir, *My Beloved World*.

2022   Sotomayor becomes the most senior member of the Supreme Court's liberal minority.

SOURCE NOTES ———————————

9 Sonia Sotomayor, *My Beloved World*, New York: Knopf, 2013, p. 288.

9 Sotomayor, p. 288.

9 Sotomayor, p. 288.

10 Sotomayor, p. 290.

20 Sotomayor, p. 237.

23 Lauren Collins, "Number Nine," *The New Yorker*, January 11, 2010, https://www.newyorker.com /magazine/2010/01/11/number-nine.

24 Elie Mystal, "How Sonia Sotomayor Became the Conscience of the Supreme Court," *The Nation*, August 22, 2022, https://www.thenation.com /article/politics/sonia-sotomayor-liberal-justice.

25 "Remarks on the Nomination of Sonia Sotomayor To Be a Supreme Court Associate Justice," The American Presidency Project, May 26, 2009, https:// www.presidency.ucsb.edu/documents/remarks-the -nomination-sonia-sotomayor-be-supreme-court -associate-justice.

27 Jeffrey Rosen, "The Case Against Sotomayor," *The New Republic*, May 3, 2009, https://newrepublic .com/article/60740/the-case-against-sotomayor.

27–28 Irin Carmon, "Reintroducing Sonia Sotomayor," *New York*, February 3, 2021, https://nymag.com /intelligencer/article/reintroducing-sonia -sotomayor.html.

28 Collins.

32 Mystal.

33–34 Adam Liptak, "Sotomayor Says Supreme Court Can 'Regain the Public's Confidence,'" *New York Times*, June 16, 2022, https://www.nytimes.com /2022/06/16/us/sonia-sotomayor-supreme-court .html.

39 Devin Dwyer, "Justice Sotomayor Gives Pep Talk to Progressives While Praising Clarence Thomas," *ABC News*, June 16, 2022, https://abcnews. go.com /Politics/justice-sotomayor-pep-talk-progressives -praising-clarence-thomas/story?id=85446415.

39 Dwyer.

SELECTED BIBLIOGRAPHY

"Background on Sonia Sotomayor." The White House, May 26, 2009. https://obamawhitehouse.archives.gov /the-press-office/background-judge-sonia-sotomayor.

Carmon, Irin. "Reintroducing Sonia Sotomayor." *New York*, February 3, 2021. https://nymag.com/intelligencer /article/reintroducing-sonia-sotomayor.html.

Collins, Lauren. "Number Nine." *The New Yorker*, January 11, 2010. https://www.newyorker.com/magazine/2010 /01/11/number-nine.

Fontana, David. "The People's Justice?" *The Yale Law Journal Forum*, March 24, 2014. https://www.yalelawjournal.org /pdf/5.Fontana_FINAL_a929e736.pdf.

Mystal, Elie. "How Sonia Sotomayor Became the Conscience of the Supreme Court." *The Nation*, August 22, 2022. https://www.thenation.com/article /politics/sonia-sotomayor-liberal-justice.

Parrot-Sheffer, Chelsey. "Sonia Sotomayor." *Britannica*. Accessed September 29, 2022. https://www.britannica .com/biography/Sonia-Sotomayor.

Sotomayor, Sonia. *My Beloved World*. New York: Knopf, 2013.

Stolberg, Sheryl Gay. "Sotomayor, a Trailblazer and a Dreamer." *New York Times*, May 26, 2009. https://www.nytimes.com/2009/05/27/us/politics/27websotomayor.html.

Toobin, Jeffrey. *The Oath: the Obama White House and the Supreme Court*. New York: Doubleday, 2012.

Wheeler, Lydia. "Sotomayor Takes the Lead as Dissenter for Embattled Liberal Justices." *Bloomberg Law*, July 5, 2022. https://news.bloomberglaw.com/us-law-week/sotomayor-takes-lead-as-dissenter-for-embattled-liberal-justices.

LEARN MORE ⎯⎯⎯⎯⎯

Abramson, Jill. *What Is the Supreme Court?* New York: Penguin Workshop, 2022.

Ahrens, Niki. *Sonia Sotomayor: First Latina Supreme Court Justice.* Minneapolis: Lerner Publications, 2022.

Britannica Kids: United States Government
https://kids.britannica.com/kids/article/United-States
-Government/353887

15 Influential Hispanic Americans Who Made History
https://www.biography.com/news/notable-hispanic
-americans

Menéndez, Juliet. *Latinitas: Celebrating 40 Big Dreamers.* New York: Godwin Books, 2021.

The Supreme Court of the United States
https://www.supremecourt.gov/about/about.aspx

INDEX

PHOTO ACKNOWLEDGMENTS

Image credits: Eric Lee/Bloomberg/Getty Images, p. 2; Paul Morigi/Getty Images, p. 6; WDC Photos/Alamy Stock Photo, p. 8; The White House/Handout/Getty Images, p. 11; The White House/Handout/Getty Images, p. 12; CBS Photo Archive/Getty Images, p. 14; WhiteHouse.gov/Wikimedia Commons (CC BY 3.0), p. 15; UPI Photo/White House Press Office/Alamy Stock Photo, p. 16; Karjean Levine/Getty Images, p. 18; AP Photo/Mark Lennihan, p. 21; Carlos Avila Gonzalez/ The San Francisco Chronicle/Hearst Newspapers/Getty Images, p. 22; Chip Somodevilla/Staff/Getty Images, p. 26; REUTERS/ Joshua Roberts/Alamy Stock Photo, p. 28; Mark Wilson/Staff/ Getty Images, p. 29; Andrew Harrer/Bloomberg/Getty Images, p. 33; Craig F. Walker/The Denver Post/Getty Images, p. 34; AP Photo/Carolyn Kaster, p. 36; Olivier Douliery/AFP/Getty Images, p. 37; Bebeto Matthews/Pool/Getty Images, p. 38.

Cover: WDC Photos/Alamy Stock Photo.